'I have called you friends'

Suggestions for the spiritual life based on the farewell discourses of Jesus

REINHARD KÖRNER OCD

SLG Press
Convent of the Incarnation Fairacres
Parker Street Oxford OX4 1TB England

www.slgpress.co.uk

First published by SLG Press, 2012

ISBN   978-0-7283-0196-2
ISSN   0307-1405

Texts translated from:
P. Reinhard Körner, *Mystik konkret*, 1998
P. Reinhard Körner, *Die Zeit ist reif*, 2005
© St. Benno-Verlag, Leipzig, www.st-benno.de
Used with permission.

Translation and cover illustration:

Printed by
Will Print   Oxford   England

CONTENTS

TRANSLATOR'S PREFACE   *page* v

1. **Friendship with God:**
   About the cover picture:
   a simple sculpture as a model of Christian life   1

2. **The farewell discourses:**
   Jesus shares the deep concerns of his heart   3

   How the discourses came to be written   3
   The prayerful character of the discourses   4
   The discourses and the threefold way   5

3. **The commandment to love:**
   The way of love   8

   The love which makes servants into friends   8
   Love is a gift   8
   The presence of divine love   9
   Love does not allow itself to be barricaded in   10
   The challenge of love   12

4. **The Holy Spirit as Teacher and Advocate:**
   God speaks all the time   14

   Jesus promises the Holy Spirit   14
   Wisdom pointing us towards the truth   15
   The Holy Spirit in our lives   16
   The Holy Spirit isn't confined within narrow boundaries 19
   Holy fresh air   21
   Three Old Testament ways of responding to truth   21
   God really speaks   24
   Becoming more attentive to the voice of God   25

5. **God as Abba, Father:**
   From servants to friends, from friends to sons and daughters 29

    An Abba-God as Father   29
    Good fortune   31
    True dignity   33
    Taking the decisive step from servant or handmaid   35

6. **Jesus and the image of the Vine:**
   Abiding in love   36

    An image of purgation   36
    Staying in relationship   37
    Turning towards God   37
    Taking seriously our faith that God is there   39

7. **A way of life in relationship with God:**
   Jesus prays for our union with God   41

    'Jesus looked up to heaven and said ...'   41
    'that they may all be one'   41
    'as you, Father, are in me, and I am in you'   42
    'may they also be in us'   44
    'so that the world may believe that you have sent me'   44
    'the glory that you have given me, I have given them'   45
    'that they may become completely one'   47
    'so that the world may know that you have loved them,
        even as you have loved me'   49
    'Father, I desire that those also ...'   50

TRANSLATOR'S PREFACE

MANY THEMES intertwine in this book, but the predominant theme is that of friendship with God, friendship with Jesus, as taught by Jesus himself in the farewell discourses handed down to us in Chapters 14 to 17 of the Gospel of John. Dr Reinhard Körner, a member of the Carmelite Order, runs the Carmelite retreat house at Birkenwerder, north of Berlin. For many years he has led retreats, presented talks and given spiritual guidance. He has written a large number of books. The first of his teaching to be published in the English language is the book *Suffering: Why all this suffering? What do I do about it?* from SLG Press (2006), a translation of two addresses given on Good Friday and Holy Saturday in 2004.

The present book is the second to appear. The author has written and said many things in the context of the farewell discourses of Jesus, and they have been collected together here. The book has been compiled, translated and edited by myself from various published writings and from talks circulated as recordings on CDs. Some chapters relate more specifically to Jesus himself, or to the Holy Spirit, or to the Father. The final chapter (Chapter 7) is a detailed reflection upon the words of the farewell or high priestly prayer, echoing the reflective nature of that prayer in John's Gospel.

The idea for the book came as I listened to the recordings of some addresses in which Fr Körner speaks of the Holy Spirit (see Chapter 4). It seemed to me that his message, so completely simple and so utterly inspiring, was itself the Holy Spirit speaking. I felt that this needed to be communicated, to be made available.

Reinhard Körner is a gifted teacher, and he has so many new ideas that it would be difficult to sum up his teaching and reduce it to any single aspect. Nevertheless, the traditional Carmelite spiritual path of 'friendship with Jesus' is a good place to begin. The author has taught me that this is what matters. Jesus is the Way, the Truth and the Life. In developing a deep, personal relationship with him, we come to the Father. Jesus promises us the gift of the Spirit. This is eternal life.

My thanks are due to Fr Reinhard Körner for sharing my enthusiasm for this book and for his trust. I should also like to thank those who have given me their support and encouragement, in particular Oblate Sister Evelyn Silouana SLG, the Reverend Bernhard Schünemann and Sister Jane OCD.

SISTER AVIS MARY SLG
Fairacres, February 2012

1.

Friendship with God

About the cover picture:
a simple sculpture as a model of Christian life

'I have called you friends.'[1]

ANYONE APPROACHING the Carmelite priory and retreat house at Birkenwerder, north of Berlin, can see from the road a little stone grotto in the garden containing a 'sculpture' made from wooden beams (see the picture on the cover). Designed and made by the brothers at the priory, it is hardly an epoch-making work of art, but it can speak to those prepared to engage with it.

The smaller figure on the left depicts St Teresa of Avila († 1582), the reformer and founder of the Carmelite Order, and the brown and cream colours are reminiscent of the brown habit and white mantle of Elijah worn by Carmelites. The larger figure on the right in green, the colour of life, symbolizes Christ, the one who is alive and present with us today.

The composition of the two figures expresses an essential feature of the life and spiritual message of St Teresa, which can be summarized as being turned in friendship with Jesus Christ towards people and the world. In an era when in religious circles more attention was paid to forms of prayer than to the one to whom the prayers were addressed, in an era which was more concerned with getting prayer requests relating to personal and church matters heard than with God, and when the faithful went in fear and trembling for their own salvation, St Teresa discovers God as the Friend of her life in Jesus, the Word made flesh. After more than twenty years in the religious life, she discovers that she can live with

---
[1] John 15: 15.

1

him 'as with a friend, a brother and companion'. It radically changes her entire existence. She gains a new understanding of her spiritual path in the religious life and of her mistakes and weaknesses and those of others, and a new understanding of the Church and of the world, of prayer and the spiritual life. Everything takes on a new backdrop when faith becomes real friendship and when prayer is 'nothing else than an intimate sharing between friends' which 'means taking time frequently to be alone with him who we know loves us'.[2]

The sculpture in the grotto is an attempt to express visually something of this mystery of friendship with Jesus, and at the same time to show that such friendship is not turned in upon itself. St Teresa tackles the tasks of everyday life together with Jesus, remains open to the world surrounding her together with him, goes out towards other people with him. Through the arms of both of them extended outwards, anyone standing before the sculpture can feel taken up into this friendship. Faith, according to St Teresa's experience, does not have its end in adoration of God, but it grows beyond that to union with God, which according to her testimony and that of many Christian mystics always includes union with God in action, turning with God towards God's creation. Teresa also learned this message from her companion in the spiritual life and our father in the Carmelite Order, St John of the Cross († 1591), in their years together in Avila. He had himself learned this fundamental principle of the spiritual life by observing the very life of the triune God, a life within which two are always one in their love for the third.

Faced with the many questions and concerns of the Church and society of her time—which are not so very different from ours—St Teresa knew that, 'together, Lord, You and I are always in the majority!'

---

[2] *Life* of St Teresa, 8: 5.

2.

The farewell discourses

Jesus shares the deep concerns of his heart

'Little children, I am with you only a little longer.'[3]

How the discourses came to be written

THE SO-CALLED farewell discourses of Jesus occupy several chapters in the Gospel of John (chapters 13-17). On the night before he was arrested and executed, Jesus sits together with his disciples at supper for the last time. First we are told about the foot washing, and then that Jesus addressed the disciples. Obviously, there was no shorthand writer in the room where the Last Supper was held, taking down some four and a half chapters at Jesus' dictation, and the words in the Gospel cannot be the actual ones used. Despite this, Christians have never been in any doubt that the words express the fundamental concerns of Jesus, and they are made all the more precious by the fact that they also bear the hallmark of the experiences and convictions of one of the early Christian communities. They are like a testament, containing not only the bequest of Jesus to his friends, but also the bequest of some of our brothers and sisters of that time to all subsequent generations in the Church. It is with an almost testamentary effect that the Johannine Christ adjures his hearers, 'Abide in me as I abide in you.'[4]

In order to understand our texts better, it helps to recall that the Gospel of John was late in coming into being, towards the end of the first century, or 60 to 70 years after the events of that last evening. The Gospel writer or writers in the community of John belonged to a later generation than the

---

[3] John 13: 33.
[4] John 15: 4.

3

Apostles. They summarized what had remained intact and had taken root in this community from what had been handed down about Jesus, and this included the farewell discourses at the end.

The texts were not simply written sitting down at a writing desk; perhaps a group of third and even fourth generation Christians sat together to write down their ideas about this time with Jesus on the evening before he suffered, when Jesus knew it would be the last occasion on which he would be together with his disciples on earth. These Christians included in the Gospel what had been passed on and what they imagined Jesus had said and what—at least in essence—he really did say. They also allowed to flow into these texts their own experience of what it was like to live as Jesus had taught them. It was, therefore, not only Jesus standing behind these texts, but also several generations of Christians who had tried to live in his spirit. They had tried to summarize Jesus' chief concerns, the deep concerns of his heart, so to speak, and they must also have used and woven in words from the whole of his life. These texts are not a catechism in which everything making up the Christian faith is carefully listed point by point. Jesus was not trying to bring us some religious philosophy, but to show us a new way of living, a way he himself lived.

The prayerful character of the discourses

Throughout the Gospel of John, the words of Jesus have a particularly prayerful character. The great spiritual teachers throughout Christian history, the praying people of Christianity, have always sensed this. St John of the Cross knew two books of the Bible by heart: from the Old Testament, the Song of Songs, and from the New Testament, the book which was particularly dear to him, the Gospel of John. There is probably a connection here with the fact that, according to our current understanding, the community within which the Gospel of John was written down was founded by the disciple referred to in this Gospel as 'the disciple whom Jesus loved'.[5] No name is ever given for this disciple. Although we have always taken it to be the Apostle John, there is some speculation in modern research that it might have been the Apostle Andrew. What is relevant here, however, is that the community was probably founded by and received its faith from a disciple by whom Jesus knew himself to be particularly deeply understood—with whom, as we would say today, he was on the same wavelength. That disciple would have understood deeply both what Jesus desired at the time, and what he as the Resurrected One continues to desire.

The discourses and the threefold way

In the Christian spiritual tradition, there is the concept of the threefold way (*triplex via*) of following Christ, which can be linked in with the farewell discourses, unfolding these discourses for both individuals and communities on their faith journey. As the ancient spiritual teachers say, it is a way of illumination (*via illuminativa*), a way of purification (*via purgativa*) and a way of union (*via unitiva*). We meet this triad in some of the early theologians, above all in Pseudo-Dionysius the Areopagite (5th century), and then more expressly in Bonaventura (13th century), in John Tauler (14th century) and in St John of the Cross (16th century). It did not mean three separate ways to God, or—as the Neo-Platonist Pseudo-Dionysius thought—steps or stages of the way which flow into one another, but—as St Bonaventura and St John of

---

[5] In the Gospel of John, it was this disciple who asked Jesus during the Last Supper who it was who would betray him. Simon Peter motioned to 'one of his disciples—the one whom Jesus loved' to ask Jesus this question (John 13: 23 ff.). Later, at the crucifixion, to 'the disciple whom he loved' Jesus said, 'Here is your mother' (John 19: 26-27). When Mary Magdalene discovered the empty tomb, she ran to tell Simon Peter and the disciple 'whom Jesus loved', and they then ran to the tomb and 'saw and believed' (John 20: 2-10).

the Cross[6] in particular made clear—these were three aspects of one threefold Christian journey of faith, and they belong together. Further reference will be made to the illuminative way (Chapter 5), the purgative way (Chapter 6) and the unitive way (Chapter 7).

In these farewell discourses, Jesus tells his disciples that there will be great pain for them when he is no longer with them, but that their pain will be turned into joy. He uses the image of a woman about to give birth who must undergo the pains of childbirth. All that is forgotten after the birth.[7] He promises that he will ask the Father, and the Father will give them 'another Advocate', 'the Spirit of truth.'[8] It is fundamental to the message of Jesus that he will rise again, that he will be with the Father and that we shall be with him. He in effect says to them: 'I shall remain with you, even if I am about to be killed. I shall not fall out of God's hands. I shall be alive with God. Though hidden, I shall go on being present. Think in the way I do. Stay connected with me.' Jesus also uses the image of the vine.[9] He says, 'I am the true vine, and my Father is the vine-grower. … Abide in me as I abide in you. Just as the branch cannot bear fruit in itself unless it abides in the vine, neither can you unless you abide in me.' Just as the branch must 'abide' in the vine so that it may bear fruit, so we should 'abide' in inner connectedness with Jesus, in a deep interior relationship with him—not just in remembrance that he once lived. He goes on to say, 'I do not call you servants any longer … but I have called you friends.'[10] Finally in these

---

[6] Above all in the *Ascent of Mount Carmel* and the *Dark Night*.
[7] See John 16: 21.
[8] John 14: 16-17.
[9] John 15: 1 ff.
[10] John 15: 15.

discourses, there comes the farewell or high priestly prayer of Jesus.[11]

Let us now take a fresh look at this bequest of Jesus, at this summary of the deepest concerns of his heart, taking a few passages and reflecting upon them in more detail.

---

[11] John 17.

3.

The commandment to love

The way of love

'This is my commandment, that you love one another, as I have loved you.'[12]

The love which makes servants into friends

'I DO NOT CALL you servants any longer ... but I have called you friends.' We shall explore this statement further in Chapter 5. It was prefaced by the writer or writers of the Gospel of John with what amounted to a programme for living, one affirmed many times by Jesus: 'This is my commandment, that you love one another as I have loved you.'[13] Since this injunction is laid down as a norm and is the key to understanding Jesus' new image of the human person, it would seem appropriate to look more closely at this word 'love'. The love which makes servants into friends, into creatures who have become fully mature sons and daughters addressed personally by God, is a love which 'goes the whole hog' in the same way as the love between two people can do. It would be utterly foolish to think any less of the all-embracing God YHWH, 'I am who I am', and once Jesus of Nazareth has opened our eyes, we can no longer do so.

Love is a gift

Love is first of all a gift, a present, unearned and not owned. As with all of God's gifts, it is to be experienced and received as a reality which is just there without our doing anything to

---

[12] John 15: 12.
[13] *ibid.* See also: John 13: 34 and 15: 17; cf. also: Mark 12: 31; Matt. 19: 19; Luke 10: 27; Eph. 5:2; Col. 3: 14, etc.

make it happen, in the same way as the air we breathe and the earth which bears us are there. Jesus opened people's eyes to this, and he showed them what love was before he gave the command to love: an indicative preceded his imperative, a message preceded his command, an invitation to believe in love preceded his challenge to love. The Protestant writer and theologian Jörg Zink writes:

> In Jesus' dealings with people, he always first of all accepts them and invites them, raises them up and encourages them, and gives them a home in the community of the sons and daughters of God. He lets them count for something. He tells them stories in which they figure, and in which they are shown who or what, according to God's purposes, they can be. He shows them a way forward and sends them away at peace. The sequence is always clear. Jesus first bestows freedom, then he issues a directive: first comes the dignity, then the commandment; first the power, then the task; first the chance of life, then the expectation; first the image of what they are to become, then the demand to do something themselves. What God does always comes first, what people can or should do afterwards.[14]

Everyone who loves knows that there is something wrong with love when an imperative is needed. A person who knows himself or herself to be loved *wants* to love. When Jesus says, 'Love one another, as I have loved you', he is asking this of his circle of friends, rather than issuing a command with raised forefinger.

The presence of divine love

God's love is no less real than human love. St John of the Cross wrote songs about it, describing it as a power which God 'poured in' to the whole creation. It hides in the mountains and in the rivers, in plants and animals, in the

---

[14] *Die Urkraft des Heiligen. Christlicher Glaube im 21. Jahrhundert,* Jörg Zink, Kreuz-Verlag, Stuttgart, 2003, p. 393.

'woods and thickets, planted by the hand of the Beloved'[15] and in the soul, 'even though it may be that of the greatest sinner in the world'.[16] For us human beings, as the Spanish Carmelite writes, it is inherent in our capacity for perception. We experience love as being touched by beauty, as being touched by what is deep, essential and precious, as being drawn to the other and wanting to say 'You' to him or her, as passion which penetrates the spirit, soul and body, as the 'Yes' to life. It is there; it only has to be 'seen'. It comes towards me from human beings and creatures, and—once I have become sensitive to it—from the God who is 'in all things' (St Ignatius of Loyola) and who is also in myself, hidden and present and waiting for us all.

Love, once discovered, becomes energy. For St John of the Cross, love (together with faith and hope) is a power given by God, which is poured into the soul's capacity for action. From there—it is always the same love—it moves out towards God, towards people and towards creatures, towards everything which is precious and worthy of love. The power to love is, according to St John of the Cross, the 'instrument' which the Creator has put into the heart of the human person, the image of the Creator, who will 'show [the soul] how it works by operating it jointly with her'.[17] In its pure form, love wants to give where something is lacking; it wants to awaken where possibilities of life have fallen asleep; it gives attention and respect, in that it gazes wonderingly. It does not then need to be summoned up through a command.

Love does not allow itself to be barricaded in

With these ideas and convictions, St John of the Cross was not trying to mislead himself or anyone else into thinking that this world is a healthy, sound one. Along with St Paul, he

---

[15] *Spiritual Canticle* B, stanza 4.
[16] *Ascent of Mount Carmel*, II 5:3.
[17] *Spiritual Canticle* 38: 4.

sees the whole creation 'groaning in labour pains'.[18] It is not perfect. Groaning inwardly, it awaits the completion which, in the form of longing, it already bears within itself.[19] And the human person has a share in all of this. The divine Sculptor is still at work, says the mystic and pastor St John of the Cross.[20] The stone which the Sculptor lovingly hews and looks upon, and looks upon and hews, already holds the potential for guessing at the precious sculpture which will come into being. Yet the Sculptor's work of art—which the Bible calls 'Adam' (Earthling)—still has many rough edges and corners. Love—'having looked at them with his image alone'[21]—has already been sculpted into Adam, but is still in conflict with all that is actually 'nothing' in comparison with it. The human person lives in a tension between the constraints of desire, which capture, seize and want to hold on, and the 'gentle breeze' of love, which gives freedom, brings out into a broad place and allows to breathe. Between these two things, there can be fear, imprisonment, longing kept behind bars, narrowness, hemming in and sometimes degeneration, instead of transformation through formation by love.

For the singer of the Dark Night, his nocturnal flight from the monastery prison of Toledo became an image for flight from such a prison. As is said in these stanzas, love—which does not permit itself to be barricaded in through narrowness and fear—is itself 'the light' which guides 'more surely than the light of noon' to the place where 'with his gentle hand' the 'breeze' of freedom blows, wherein the 'Lover and his beloved' find their way to one another.[22]

---

[18] Rom. 8: 22.
[19] cf. Rom. 8: 23.
[20] cf. *Counsels to a Religious on How to Reach Perfection*, 3.
[21] *Spiritual Canticle B*, Stanza 5.
[22] *Dark Night of the Soul*, Stanzas.

The challenge of love

Pope John Paul II, who as a young priest wrote his doctoral thesis on St John of the Cross, said: 'I believe that in order to understand the greatness of the human person, one must assimilate the theology of St John of the Cross, the view of being human which his teaching opens up; one can then no longer forget one's own dignity.'[23]

Texts like the Song of Songs, poems like those of St John of the Cross and verses written by lovers of all times awaken what is always already deep within us human beings. The 'voice from outside', St Augustine says, awakens the 'voice from within'. It gives, as St John of the Cross is aware, 'no increase to the soul; it only brings to light what was previously possessed that she may have enjoyment of it'.[24] What awakens there is that same voice which Jesus once awakened in the rich and the poor, in the devout and the hypocrites, of Galilee and Jerusalem, when he told them about the Kingdom of God which is 'among you'.[25] It is this voice of love, poured in by the Creator and awakened by Jesus which—when all the strong men in the circle of disciples had taken flight—drove Mary of Magdala to the grave of the Beloved, and which in the end gave her the certainty of the Resurrection. It is always the same love, the love which also gives me the overwhelming confidence that in the end God will simply not allow my life—and all that is loved by God and by me—to fall into nothingness again.

Nothing challenges as much as a love like this. Threats and punishments can at most divert human beings temporarily from their evil intentions. Although it might be possible to implant fear into others' souls by such means, so that they 'avoid sin', they will then always be caught up with

---

[23] Address at the (Teresian) Institute of Spirituality in Rome, 22 April 1979.
[24] *Spiritual Canticle* 20/21: 14.
[25] Luke 17: 21.

worry as to whether it is at all possible to placate someone—a parent, a teacher, God—placed above them. Love, on the other hand, changes people, allows them to mature, becoming life-giving energy and allowing each one to become who he or she really is. Everyone who has experienced love, even if only to some extent, knows that no adventure in life is greater and more profitable than such love. It is worth building one's entire existence upon it. Only people who know themselves to be utterly and completely loved, affirmed and accepted— irrespective of achievements and without having earned it— will be able to love. They can then allow others their own validity, ascribing dignity to the other and even rejoicing in him or her from the heart—because they do not have to struggle and fear for their own dignity.

4.

The Holy Spirit as Teacher and Advocate

God speaks all the time

'The Spirit of truth ... will guide you into all the truth.'[26]

Jesus promises the Holy Spirit

AS I BEGAN my theological training leading to the priesthood in 1965, there was a great deal of talk about the Holy Spirit. The Second Vatican Council was just coming to an end, and everyone was expecting the Holy Spirit to bring about a renewal in the Church. Looking back now over the decades, I think that although much renewal has taken place, in many respects we could say that the Holy Spirit might have blown a bit more powerfully through the Church!

Nowhere else in the New Testament is the Holy Spirit spoken about so frequently and in so concentrated and detailed a manner as in the farewell discourses. Jesus says, 'I will ask the Father, and he will give you another Advocate, to be with you for ever. This is the Spirit of truth.'[27] The Father will give us an Advocate. The word used in the Greek is *parakletos*. The Paraclete is literally one who is a help and support to us, who is at our side and accompanies us, who stands by us: an Advocate.

Jesus continues, 'The Advocate, the Holy Spirit, whom the Father will send in my name, will teach you everything, and remind you of all that I have said to you.'[28] In this context, being *reminded* means not just having things brought to our

---

[26] John 16: 13.
[27] John 14: 16-17.
[28] John 14: 26.

14

minds, but also interiorizing them, which leads to under-standing at a deeper level. Jesus goes on to say, 'When the Spirit of truth comes, he will guide you into all the truth.'[29] The Holy Spirit, then, is a companion who teaches us the truth, who leads us into the truth and enables us to under-stand the truth more deeply, reminding us of all that Jesus has said. We may see this action of the Holy Spirit as one of the aspects of the threefold way mentioned in Chapter 2, namely the way of illumination or the *via illuminativa*. Those wishing to travel the way of Jesus and make his way of life their own must open the self, listening to the 'illuminations' of the Spirit of truth who will guide them 'into all truth'.

Jesus even says—and those who write this down in the Gospel know it from their own experience—'I tell you the truth: it is to your advantage that I go away, for if I do not go away, the Advocate will not come to you; but if I go, I will send him to you.'[30]

Wisdom pointing us towards the truth

The Jewish people often used the word 'wisdom' to mean those thoughts, words, events, experiences or realities which point a person further on into the truth of life. The word occurs many times in the Old Testament. It was not used as it is sometimes used today, in the sense of the accumulation of knowledge. That is not wisdom in the biblical sense. A person can know a great deal and have studied a great deal, yet still lack wisdom. Nor does wisdom mean having an unusually high intelligence quotient. Ordinary people, including children, can be wise in the biblical sense. In the German language, the root of the word *Weisheit*, wisdom, is not the verb *wissen*, meaning 'to know', but rather the verb *weisen*, 'to point'. Wisdom is not something which I possess, but it is ahead of me, pointing me onwards and drawing my attention to

---

[29] John 16: 13.
[30] John 16: 7.

something deeper. Wisdom has an existence of its own. It is outside of myself to begin with, but I can receive it, let it in and allow it to point me onwards.

There are also texts from the early Church which refer to this Spirit who is like a teacher, bringing wisdom and truth from God. In the book of the Revelation of John—the final book in the New Testament, although it was actually written around the year 85, somewhat earlier than the Gospel of John—the same wording is repeated seven times, as penetrating wisdom for the Christian communities, 'Let anyone who has an ear listen to what the Spirit is saying to the churches.'[31]

The early Christians soon began to call this Advocate of whom Jesus speaks 'the Holy Spirit', and they meant the Spirit who brings wisdom which points us onwards towards something. If these words of Jesus and of the Gospel writers who recorded what Jesus said are not just pious words but are real, then there must be some connection with our actual experience. The question is, then, how we can discover the Holy Spirit as a reality in our lives today.

The Holy Spirit in our lives

I am convinced that we can experience this working of the Holy Spirit, and I'd like to give some specific examples of quite ordinary things of which I have myself become increasingly aware over the years. For instance, you might be in the middle of a conversation with someone, and perhaps it is someone who has you thinking, 'Oh dear! He isn't going to have anything very sensible to say!' Then he does say something which—even though you might ordinarily have little confidence in what he says—you recognise to be the truth. It may be a pleasant thought, or it may be an unwelcome or challenging one, but in any case, you know you must take notice of it. However he intended what he said, it has struck you, and you realise that if you allow in this thought, it will

---

[31] Rev. 2: 7, 11, 17, 29; 3: 6, 13, 22.

take you on further. You might not give away to him the fact that it has affected you, but afterwards you can pay attention to this wisdom pointing you towards something.

Or perhaps you have one of those calendars where you tear off a leaf daily, or every other day, or weekly, and find a new saying. It may not have texts from the Bible on it, or any religious words at all, but it has sayings which people selected because the words spoke to them. I get up in the morning, look at the calendar and read one of these sayings and think, 'Yes; that's not bad!'—and then forget it. The next day, I tear off the calendar, read another saying and have the sense instantly, 'Yes! That's true! It's as if that has been written for me. That's it! I must note it down and think about it. It might take me on a bit further.' Someone else, reading the same words on the same day will perhaps say, 'Yes; that's not bad!' just as I did the day before, or possibly even, 'That doesn't mean a thing to me!' But the saying has spoken to me.

You might be reading a book. It need not be a religious book; it might be a detective novel, for instance. You find that the first 30 pages or so are not particularly exciting, but even if the book doesn't exactly have you on the edge of your seat, it isn't so boring that you simply toss it aside. You go on reading, and then, suddenly, you come to two sentences at the bottom of page 57. You read them—and you just know: 'That's it! This really is true! This really relates to my life at this moment.' You don't want to forget them. You look quickly for a pencil and mark the passage. You read it again, perhaps copy it out. Another person might well read on without pausing over this saying at all. You might already have read the book a few years ago and passed over this passage, but now for you it is wisdom pointing you towards something ahead of you. From the perspective of the believer, this is the Holy Spirit, the Spirit who wants to lead us into the truth of our lives.

Let us look at another way we all know in which truth can come to us and point us onwards. I'm sitting on the bus going to the shops, or at my desk working, and I look dreamily out of the window. A thought passes through my mind, and another one—and then suddenly a particular thought comes and I just know: 'Yes! That's true!' It could have been the outcome of something I was reflecting upon, or something I had been thinking about in passing, or perhaps it was suddenly there without my having really thought about it at all. Anyway, a thought has now come to me which I know is true and affects me, and I know I must take notice of it. I might look for a pen, so that I can write it down. I don't want to forget it. Perhaps I am faced with making a particular decision, wondering whether I should do this or that, or I have already made up my mind to do something—but then I suddenly and unexpectedly feel very uneasy. I stop for a moment. It may start as just a feeling at first, but then the piece of wisdom is expressed more and more in words. It becomes an increasing awareness within me, like an inner voice (though not an audible one), a thought which is warning me, 'Be careful! Pay attention to truth in what you are thinking of doing now! Think it over once more! Is this really the last word about it?' The inner voice may even become more insistent than that: 'Don't do that! If you do it, you'll be doing wrong. You'll be harming others, perhaps harming yourself.' This is the voice which we know as the voice of conscience.

It does not always have to be wisdom in a form which can be put into words. Quite often it has happened to me that I have been given a music CD as a gift, and I put it on in the evening while I'm working at my desk and listen to it playing in the background—but then suddenly I take more notice of a particular piece of music and think, 'Yes! That's wonderful!' I have to put down my pen and listen properly. I'm completely spellbound by this music. I don't know how or why, since I cannot put it into words, but this music is telling me a deep truth, a wordless one. This melody now playing addresses me amidst my cares on this evening and says to me, 'Reinhard! There are greater things...!' It can put many a care into perspective. It can lead me into a deeper level of reality, without my being able to put anything into words.

The ancients who wrote both the Old and New Testaments and many others in the history of the faith—Jesus too—say about experiences like these, 'There you have the Holy Spirit! That's the voice of the Holy Spirit, the Spirit of truth! The Holy Spirit is trying to teach you something, to lead you on further.' It was their belief that whenever a truth is standing before us, no matter whence it comes, it is from God. The Holy Spirit of God tries to speak to us and point us onwards through inspirations and intuitions which arise within us.

The Holy Spirit isn't confined within narrow boundaries

We might say, 'But those are only experiences which everyone has, not just Christians.' And of course that is so. They are part of common human experience in every age, including our own, and whether a person is religious—no matter to which religion he or she belongs—or lives without religion. They can happen to people who never go anywhere near a church. The Holy Spirit of God works not only in the Church and in our own lives, but also in the whole of humanity and in the lives of people of other faiths and of none. Even though it would not enter the head of someone who is not a Christian to say, 'The Holy Spirit is behind this', yet it is the same Spirit. God is behind experiences of pointing wisdom, no matter whence they come. Jesus speaks of that Spirit who leads us into the truth, who teaches us and reminds us and enables us to interiorize things and to go deeper. As a believer, I can recognize this. If I allow wisdom in, then it may sometimes be painful, but it always leads me further on, to deeper life. It can change something in me and in my relationships with others. It can change something in the world—both in the big world out there and in my own little world. When the bishop visits a parish to administer the sacrament of confirmation, the candidates are there waiting. 'Receive the Holy Spirit', we say. Is that real? Have the candidates not already had experiences of the Holy Spirit beforehand and acted upon them? Of course they have! The Holy Spirit has been there for a long time and was at work the previous day, and the day before that—indeed, years before. God does not *begin* sending the Spirit to the candidates at their confirmation, nor does the bishop bring along the Holy Spirit in the boot of the car! The sacrament of confirmation is a sacred sign of a reality which is always *already* there. In that case, then, why do we have confirmation—or indeed, why be a Christian at all? The answer is that we receive the sacrament of confirmation as Christians so that we may be helped to become more aware of the presence of the Holy Spirit of God in our lives and to recognize what is happening in the depths.

At confirmation we receive the assurance that the Spirit of God *will* speak to us again and again, and we are enabled to become more sensitive to this Companion who wants to lead us ever more deeply into the truth of life. Becoming more sensitive to God working in ourselves and in all people will enable us to avoid becoming 'church people'—not at all the same thing as being Christians! 'Church people' look at the Church with blinkers, as if God and the Spirit only work within the Church, but Christians, once they have really discovered the Holy Spirit in the Church, see God's Spirit at work everywhere. Where truth is, there is the Spirit of God.

Holy fresh air

Jesus' native language was Aramaic, a common form of Hebrew at the time. The word which Jesus used for the Spirit of God, for the Holy Spirit, was common to both Hebrew and Aramaic: *Ruach*. It was the word used by everyone in this context, but it was not a specifically religious word. It was also used for the breath which keeps people alive. It meant something like 'fresh air'. This could be a gentle breeze or a powerful wind, but it brought refreshment and enabled people to breathe out again. If the Jewish people, including Jesus, spoke of the Holy Spirit, then they were actually speaking of the holy fresh air which comes from God. Allowing the language of God, which always speaks through truth, into our lives will let in fresh air and the breath which keeps us alive. Truths may be like tender little breezes which you are glad to listen to, or they can have a way of blowing quite breathtakingly into your face, so that you don't want to get involved with them at all. However we experience them, through them, God brings fresh air and life into our personal lives, into the parish, into the Church as a whole and into the whole world.

Three Old Testament ways of responding to truth

The Old Testament contains many reflections on how to deal with the Holy Spirit who leads us into all truth. The first ten chapters of the Book of Wisdom deal expressly with possible ways of responding to experiences of wisdom. The book came into being in the century before Christ from a diaspora community in Alexandria in northern Egypt. The writers have Solomon—who ranked as the wisest of men—say, 'Wisdom is radiant and unfading, and she is easily discerned by those who love her, and is found by those who seek her.'[32] Then Solomon goes on to say, 'One who rises early to seek

---

[32] Wis. 6: 12.

her will have no difficulty, for she will be found sitting at the gate.'[33] All Solomon has to do is to open the gate and let her in. He says that when he recognized this teacher—wisdom— he sought to make her the companion of his life: 'I desired to take her for my bride.'[34] He wanted to be with her constantly: 'I determined to take her to live with me, knowing that she would give me good counsel and encouragement in cares and grief',[35] and furthermore, 'I preferred her to sceptres and thrones, and I accounted wealth as nothing in comparison with her. Neither did I liken to her any priceless gem, because all gold is but a little sand in her sight, and silver will be accounted as clay before her.'[36]

Three ways of responding to wisdom are discussed in the Book of Wisdom. We can use them to discern whether we are becoming more sensitive to wisdom and paying attention to her. The positive way is that of the wise person, and the other two are negative ways, whereby one can simply fail to deal rightly with wisdom: the way of the foolish person and the way of the evildoer.

The positive way of dealing with wisdom is embraced by people who are on the way to becoming wise. They know that they can become wiser by listening to wisdom, not just with the outer muscles of the ear, but also with the inner hearing. God's wisdom is already sitting at my gate early every morning, and I should look for her as early as possible and open the gate for her. I should then look again and again in the course of the day to see if God is trying to speak to me. I should allow wisdom to come to me and draw her into my life, reflecting on her and allowing my previously held beliefs to be challenged and modified, having the courage to think bigger and letting her take me further. If I do so, I shall

---

[33] Wis. 6: 14.
[34] Wis. 8: 2.
[35] Wis. 8: 9.
[36] Wis. 7: 8-9.

become increasingly wise and truly live with the Holy Spirit as the partner of my life. There are many prayers in the Bible which ask God for understanding and wisdom and a listening heart; for example, 'Give your servant ... an understanding mind to govern your people, able to discern between good and evil',[37] and, 'You desire truth in the inward being; therefore teach me wisdom in my secret heart.'[38] These prayers are saying to God in effect, 'Take care of me. Don't let me close the gate. Make me sensitive to wisdom when she tries to speak to me. Make sure I don't distort the truth, just because I think it would make my life easier and more comfortable.'

The second way of dealing with the Spirit of Truth is the foolish way—the way of the fool. 'Foolishness' in the Bible does not mean stupidity in the sense of having little education or knowing little, but it has to do with the way I deal with the truth. If I am foolish, it means that I do hear and I do become aware of a reality or pointing wisdom and know that I should pay attention to it and listen more closely—but then I just push it aside. I do so because truth is always something of a challenge. I might have to allow something new into myself. I might have to change my thinking, and possibly also things to which I have grown accustomed. The human person has a curious gravitational tendency towards what is familiar. If I might have to think differently, and perhaps even sometimes have to change the habits of a lifetime, then I may well think that it is better to push the truth aside and keep the gate shut—but then my Teacher is standing outside, the very Spirit of God!

I can do all this myself too. I'm not always wise—but at least it's something if I know what a fool I can be at times! Even though I might be well aware of what would be the

---

[37] 1 Kgs. 3: 9.
[38] Ps. 51: 6.

23

better step, taking me into a deeper and at the same time more conscious way of living, yet I choose to stay with that to which I have grown accustomed, and I just go on with all my foolishness. If, on the other hand, I can keep opening the gate again after all—even just a crack—then it will help me to grow and mature.

The third way of dealing with wisdom is what the Bible calls the way of the evildoer. Evildoers hear and recognize the truth—but they just do not want to perceive it. They therefore bend the truth, turning it into a lie, so that it can make no further claim on them. Evildoers invent their own truth in order not to have to alter their thinking, their habits and their lives. If they can convert the truth to a half-truth, then they are free again to continue their usual thinking on the usual tracks. This happens quite easily. When they speak, they leave out a bit of the truth here and there, and then the truth has been toned down or glossed over, and it becomes a half truth. We are also very good at doing this in the Church. We dress up a truth in pious words—and then it has been toned down! The Holy Spirit is there, pointing us onwards, yet, tragically, can do nothing with us. God does not force us, but respects our freedom as human beings.

God really speaks

These days we hear it said again and again by Christians, and sometimes by people of high standing within the Church, that in our time God has become a silent God. When people say that, what they actually mean is that people have become unable to hear the language of God. It is not that God is silent, but that people do not hear.

I shall *never* have to live with a silent God. What is asked of me, though, is that I train my hearing and try to be a person who listens. God is *not* a silent God, but speaks all the time; not audibly, but in a *language* which imparts wisdom. The more I become attentive to the Holy Spirit, the more my life and my relationship with God will become like a conversation, wherein I can learn wonderful things which go deep. Jesus in his farewell prayer prays with great longing that we may find in our lives a deep inner relationship with God, and that in caring for this inner relationship (which is what we call prayer) we shall be able to say to God all that is in our hearts. We shall consider this further in Chapter 7.

We have to train our ears for God speaking through the Spirit of truth in what presents itself to us. We shall be challenged to let ourselves into this truth; or not—sometimes we do just *demolish* the possibility for ourselves. This isn't always our fault. The Christianity in which we have become immersed is on the whole a very *active* Christianity, where what we primarily understand by prayer is the use of many words. Christianity really has become a *talking religion*! Perhaps we need to close our mouths more in our church services, so that God can speak and we can listen. In our personal prayer, too, we might start off with, for instance, 'In the Name of the Father and of the Son and of the Holy Spirit' and then off we go, perhaps with the rosary next, and then reeling off this prayer and that one—and then we get up again and leave! In our services and in our personal prayer, we talk *at* God—but God can't get anywhere near us. We know how it is in a human relationship, if from first to last the other person just talks and talks—or if I do so myself and do not listen, which is of course just as bad. People cannot really meet one another like this; it is the same in our relationship with God.

Becoming more attentive to the voice of God

How, then, can we Christians train ourselves to listen to the Holy Spirit, to the language of God in our lives? I should like to suggest some quite ordinary things. For instance, I could try a bit harder to take at least a few moments to switch off the radio, to close the door, above all to close my mouth, to become still within, thinking of God, and becoming aware of God's presence, and saying, 'God, I can't see you, but you are here, hidden. Probably you have already spoken to me today through some truth and I was not listening. I do want to open my ears again from now on. Help me to do this.' It often happens to me in such moments of silence that something comes up which is important for my life, but which could not surface because I was so busy and God could not get through to me. It does not cost us much to do this, but it does take us much further on and will affect our interpersonal relationships and everything else as well.

Another way in which I can specifically nurture this relationship with God is through becoming more aware of what I read, ensuring that what I read is good and edifying. When I'm on a train journey, I see people who, as soon as they get on the train, start leafing through glossy magazines without really reading them—and that is how they spend all the precious journey time. They might have as much as three hours, and they could be reading something sensible, but they leaf through this stuff which just does one's head in! If I know that I shall have half an hour or more, then I can take something sensible with me to read and let words speak to me which really have something to say and can help me onwards. The Christian tradition expressly upholds this, especially in the religious orders, where it is known as spiritual reading. At the priory, we have an hour a day set apart for this in the early mornings. In this time, I take some book which for the moment is providing nourishment for me. I read it, and then when I get to a place which speaks to me, I don't just go on reading, but shut the book and reflect upon it. It is like taking in nourishment. Once you have recognized what this can mean and what it can give you, then you can get quite addicted to it! At any rate, you get to know that reading something deep and good and letting some truth from the Spirit of God speak to you, so that it can help you to mature and deepen your life, is just as important as the bodily nourishment which you take in.

A further possibility is conversation with others about important and essential things. It doesn't have to be about religion, just something to do with being human, something which goes deep. I know it isn't always possible when talking with people to get onto a deep level, but sometimes it happens almost spontaneously. Many people immediately then try to change the subject, and there you are, back to the weather again! If you stay with it, listening to what the other thinks and why, you will sometimes be astonished what people can give you which is important for your own life— and the Holy Spirit is behind this.

There is also the possibility of going on a retreat, either a completely silent retreat, or one accompanied by a series of talks. At Birkenwerder, for example, we have our retreat house, where many people come during the course of the year to spend perhaps three or four days in silence. In the morning and in the afternoon there is a talk, and in the evening a brief reflection. People have the opportunity to reflect upon important issues of life and faith without being drawn away by their work or by the telephone, so that they are able to stay focussed and acquire a listening heart. If we discover the Holy Spirit in a deeper way in the course of a retreat, then after the retreat we may be able more consciously to detect and listen to the Spirit in our daily lives.

Here is one last tip as to how we may become more attentive to this language of God, who is the great partner of our lives, so that our lives may become conversation and we may learn things which are existential and real. The Spirit of God always leads us to deeper life, into life in fullness. The more attentive I am, the more aware I become that I have at my side a wonderful companion, a great Friend. We began this chapter with the words of Jesus, that he would send us this Holy Spirit, this Advocate or *parakletos* from God the

Father. Using the word 'advocate' in the legal sense, I'd like to suggest that you adopt in your lives something we often hear said these days, namely, 'I'm not prepared to do anything without consulting my lawyer'!

5.

God as Abba, Father

From servants to friends, from friends to sons and daughters

'I do not call you servants any longer, because the servant does not know what the master is doing; but I have called you friends, because I have made known to you everything that I have heard from my Father.'[39]

An Abba-God as Father

THERE ARE SOME texts with which the Church is very familiar, but which have also been so overworked or diluted that we can scarcely register them now. 'Sons and daughters' have become 'children' of God—which, though potentially full of meaning, says something and nothing. 'Brothers and sisters' often becomes merely a polite form of address, rather than something to be taken seriously. Yet these are words of scripture, the concentrated power of their origin is concealed within them, and it pays to listen to them again afresh.

Jesus addressed God as 'Father', and the word he used in Aramaic was 'Abba'. This does not simply mean 'Father'; it is the word which sons and daughters used within the family, not only as small children, but also as adults, to address their fathers. It is a word which expresses a relationship of deep trust. Jesus' use of this word 'Abba', dear Father, to speak to and about God was in complete contravention of all the customs of his time. It expresses his entire view of God. For Jesus, God is not a God who is on the whole good to people, yet also punishes them and calls them to account, so that they have to live in constant fear. Because of this distorted and ambivalent image of God which Jesus encountered (and

---

[39] John 15: 15.

which still persists today), he says: 'You must think bigger of God. You are projecting your human thinking, your human nature, onto God, in the way you think. You treat one another like this: "I'll do to you what you do to me. If you are good to me, then I'll be good to you too. If you are nasty to me, then I'll also be nasty to you." But God is not like that.' Matthew, who gathered together many important teachings of Jesus in the collection of sayings known as the Sermon on the Mount, records there that Jesus said: 'Your Father in heaven ... makes his sun rise on the evil and on the good, and sends rain on the righteous and on the unrighteous.'[40]

We do not need to live in fear and anxiety as to whether we can stand at all before God. We cannot just pretend that black is white with God, but for God we are greater than all the mischief we get up to, all the stupid things we do. This new image of God given to us by Jesus has certain consequences. This Abba, this dear Father, is a God of love without cause and without condition. If God is this Abba-God, then, as is emphasized over and over again in the writings of the New Testament, all human beings are sons and daughters of God and we are brothers and sisters in relation to one another. Just as Jesus addressing God as 'Abba' represents a revolutionary image of God, so these words also stand for a new view of the human person, another new image which came into the world with Jesus of Nazareth.

We are not mere servants and handmaids, but friends of Jesus and his Father. This is the new perception of ourselves which we have been given. Based upon this new perception of each other, our relationships with one another should also have the character of friendship. 'The friends send you their greetings. Greet the friends there, each by name',[41] writes an

---

[40] Matt. 5: 45.
[41] 3 John 1: 15.

30

elder of the community in which the Gospel of John came into being, in a letter to 'the beloved Gaius' in another community.[42]

Good fortune

We can only really understand what is new and revolutionary in these words when we consider that, in contrast to the social structure of the western European world today, it was no small thing at that time to be someone's servant or handmaid. In the old ordering of society (which is actually not all that far back in the past), servants and handmaids were like members or dependants of the family. They became a part of it for life. It was an honour not to have to eke out a miserable existence as a hired hand, but rather to be a servant in the service of a good lord and master. Against this background, we can understand how the people in both the Old and New Testaments could really count themselves as very fortunate to be a 'servant of God',[43] or a 'servant of Christ'[44] (like Paul), or a 'handmaid of the Lord'[45] (like Mary). Yet as the writer of the Gospel of John knows, Jesus was taking his disciples beyond even this honour and dignity: 'You are friends in the eyes of God! Free, on an equal footing, not inferiors!' To his servants, a lord shares out the work; with his friends, he shares his life.

The words 'son' and 'daughter' can be understood to have a similar significance. Among the people of Israel from whom the first Christians came, kings or individual 'righteous' could be described as sons of God. Through the prophet Hosea, the whole people was permitted to regard

---

[42] 3 John 1: 1.
[43] In the New Testament: Titus 1: 1; Jas. 1: 1.
[44] e.g. Rom. 1: 1; Gal. 1: 10.
[45] Luke 1: 38, 48.

31

itself as a 'son' of Yahweh,[46] not only in the sense of being created by God, but in the sense of the fatherly and caring, motherly and loving, relationship of Yahweh to the people of the covenant and its leading or spirit-filled figures. It was a high honour and dignity to belong to a people which was a 'son'. Now, however, being a son applied no longer only to the people as a whole and to some prominent personalities within it, but to every single person among the people, to every man and woman, to every elderly person and child. 'God sent his Son ... so that we might receive adoption as children. And because you are children, God has sent the Spirit of his Son into our hearts, crying "Abba! Father!"'[47] says Paul to the Galatians. The Greek word *hyioi* ('sons'; in modern translations 'children') includes both sons and daughters of God. Paul reminds the Christians in Rome in similar words of this new image of humanity introduced by Jesus: 'For all who are led by the Spirit of God are children of God. For you did not receive a spirit of slavery to fall back into fear, but you have received a spirit of adoption. When we cry, "Abba! Father!" it is that very Spirit bearing witness with our spirit that we are children of God.'[48]

That applies even if the son becomes a 'prodigal' son[49] who is only able to say, 'Father ... I am no longer worthy to be called your son; treat me like one of your hired hands.' The son ended up with the pigs, yet is awaited with outstretched arms. The father runs to meet him: 'In eastern conditions, this was out of the ordinary, yes, virtually scandalous.'[50] He kisses him, clothes him with the best robe and holds a feast for him.

---

[46] Hos. 11: 1: 'When Israel was a child, I loved him, and out of Egypt I called my son.'
[47] Gal. 4: 4-6.
[48] Rom. 8: 14 ff.
[49] Luke 15: 11-32.
[50] *Stuttgarter Neues Testament: Einheitsübersetzung mit Kommentar und Erklärungen*, Stuttgart 2000, 152.

Admittedly it was a precondition that the son recognized his misdoing and confessed sincerely to the one whom he had wronged, 'Father, I have sinned against heaven and before you.' Only then can the father forgive. And then true reconciliation—not just an easy sweeping of things under the carpet—takes place. Not only does the father show mercy, but he *heals* with his love and understanding. The son truly becomes a son again. The ring which the father puts onto the hand of the one who has come home isn't just some expensive piece of jewellery, but the signet ring; the son is thereby put once more on a par with the father.

True dignity

According to Jesus' image of the human being, a person— even one who has done wrong—is a beloved son or daughter of God, not in the state of development of an immature child, but taken seriously and recognized as having the dignity of an adult. 'Think bigger of God', Jesus says. 'God can only be the highest love! And think bigger of yourselves. The God of unconditional love has you in mind!' He says: 'Look at the birds of the air; they neither sew nor reap nor gather into barns, and yet your heavenly Father feeds them. Are you not of more value than they?'[51] You are of far more value!

Probably most Christians have not yet entirely heard who they really are. As they don't know the Abba of unconditional love, neither do they know their own true dignity. Under the burden of their ambivalent image of God, many prefer to eke out a hired hand's existence before God, all their lives striving to gain through prayer, sacrifice, attendance at church services and charitable works the attention for which they long and pray. Some are convinced that they are more or less fulfilling their religious duties faithfully and sincerely. Others have the constant feeling of being fundamentally far too awful for a real spiritual life (as they understand it). Or, if God has lost all

---

[51] Matt. 6: 26.

appeal for them, then they get their daily wage from elsewhere, thinking: 'Well, God will understand.' It doesn't even occur to them—because they aren't actually living with God—that God suffers from their misery and waits for them longingly, like the father in the Parable of the Prodigal Son.

There are also the servants and handmaids among us. These are the ones, whether faithful lay Christians or clergy, who know themselves to be completely taken up by God 'in the Lord's service', and they find a certain fulfilment in that. These are dedicated people, filled with zeal for God, but also plagued with self doubts, uncertainties, feelings of guilt and fears of failure. Some cover this up in holding offices and titles, but thereby simply betray themselves. Others suffer in silence, but in doing so they go around presenting a distorted picture of people who have been 'saved'. I meet all this constantly in my retreat and pastoral work.

And all this affects one's attitude towards one's fellow human beings. A person who lives as a hired hand will only see hired hands around, will have little understanding of the servant, and even less of the son and daughter, and in the best case will gaze from afar at what he or she is unable to be. Pharisaical arrogance or feelings such as envy will determine relationships with others. Even if a person speaks of having 'brothers and sisters', yet he or she will not develop a true sense of brotherhood and sisterhood. For someone who is God's servant, only servants will be allowed to count. Free people will seem threatening. If the truth lived by sons and daughters cannot be blotted out, then, in order to neutralize the challenge they present, they'll be explained away as people 'endowed with exceptional graces'. (Many a person has been rendered safe, made unthreatening, by being 'raised to the honour of the altars'![52])

---

[52] [Editorial note: This refers to the beatification by the Roman Catholic Church of a person who has died, a step in the process leading towards canonization (i.e. of declaring him or her to be a saint). Beatification is

Taking the decisive step from servant or handmaid

We are told in the most ancient and unadulterated tradition of the Church, as it has been handed down to us in the letters of Paul: 'For in Christ Jesus you are all children of God through faith. As many of you as were baptized into Christ have clothed yourselves with Christ. There is no longer Jew or Greek, there is no longer slave or free, there is no longer male and female, for all of you are one in Christ Jesus.'[53]

The decisive step from servant or handmaid to son or daughter and friend is one which can only be taken entirely personally by each individual. Otherwise nothing will change, in one's own life, or in Christianity as a whole. This step is a very simple one. I try to believe in the love God has for me. Even better, I not only try, but I just for once take it really seriously, that it is so. I believe it of God. I believe it of God that I am a beloved son, a beloved daughter.

I know, of course, that it can be very, very difficult to take this simple step. I've known people who were able to accomplish it in a few minutes, and once for all. Nothing was ever the same again afterwards. I know others, myself included, who have needed years to do it. At some point, and I don't myself know how, it was accomplished. And from where I am now, I don't want go back on that step!

---

the bestowal of the title of 'Blessed' and a recognition accorded by the Church of that person's accession to heaven and capacity to intercede on behalf of individuals who pray using his or her name. Masses may now be held in that person's honour, and it is to this privilege that the term 'raising to the honour of the altars' refers.]

[53] Gal. 3: 26-28.

6.

Jesus and the image of the Vine

Abiding in love

'I am the true Vine ... you are the branches ... those who abide in me ... bear much fruit. ... Abide in my love.'[54]

USING THE IMAGE of the vine, Jesus says: 'Just as the branch cannot bear fruit by itself unless it abides in the vine, neither can you unless you abide in me... because apart from me you can do nothing.'[55]

An image of purgation

We may connect the way of purgation or purification, the *via purgativa* mentioned in Chapter 2, with this Parable of the Vine, with abiding in love: 'Every branch that bears fruit, he prunes to make it bear more fruit.'[56] If anything in the New Testament presents us with a real challenge to examine our consciences, then it is this passage. Not bearing fruit at all, or not bearing enough fruit, or bearing fruit amidst withered and dried up leafage; all this precisely reflects our current situation in the Church. 'Too many material things, too little Gospel, too little living in faith', as Bishop Franz Kamphaus of Limburg put it in a sermon to the faithful of his diocese in September 2004. We have 'unequivocally' to say that 'there is not much which is appealing in what emanates from the Church'. More dangerous than the loss of external standing in society is 'the creeping secularization from within'.[57] The

---

[54] John 15: 1-11.
[55] John 15: 4-5.
[56] John 15: 2.
[57] Sermon for the Feast of the Holy Cross, Bad Schwalbach, 19 Sept. 2004, qtd. in the *Main-Rheiner*, 20 Sept. 2004.

question before us, then, to put it another way, is whether we are abiding in Jesus and he is abiding in us.

Staying in relationship

The injunction, 'abide in me and I in you' is the exhortation of the Johannine Christ to his disciples—both those of the time and those today—to remain in a personal relationship with him. No word in the original Greek text implies any condition. *Meinate en emoi, kago en hymin* does not mean abide in me, *then* I shall abide in you. Jesus has not made his abiding in us in any way conditional. His enduring presence, his friendship with every human being—which he never breaks off—is not the consequence of, or even the reward for, our abiding in him, but rather is the prerequisite for our entering into relationship with him. What is meant is a personal relationship where both sides abide in an 'I-in-You and You-in-me'. But what does this mean in practical terms? How do I abide in you and in your Abba-God, Jesus? What really *is* it that at times has been called the 'way of union'?

Turning towards God

We do have to take some step along a path. It is the same step which people have to take in order to enter into and live in a relationship with another person. I have to look at the other person, turn towards him or her, speak, listen, spend time together with that person. This is what we also have to do with God, but the difference is that God is always the partner who is both hidden and present, the one in whom we believe. Uniting myself with God means that I turn towards God and think about God being there—albeit hidden from sensory perception—and I say consciously, 'You, God...' I talk to God, spend time in God's presence—with and without words—and listening rather than speaking.

That is all there is to it, but we cannot omit this step on the Christian journey of faith. A loving turning of oneself towards God is the prerequisite for a committed relationship with God. When this looking at or attending to God becomes habitual, it changes having an outward faith into believing in God as a living person. The great spiritual teachers try to guide others towards this. The command to love God—which had already been called for in the credo of Israel and was affirmed by Jesus—is realized not in the worship of God, as this, be it ever so splendid, remains external, but in this 'fundamental act of faith'[58] (St Thomas Aquinas).

To describe this fundamental act of faith, St John of the Cross uses the expression *advertencia amorosa*, which means something like turning towards God, lovingly, and borne up by confidence in divine love. According to John's concept of the human person, union with God is not something to be attained. From God's perspective, it is always there already, since 'God sustains every soul and dwells in it substantially, even though it may be that of the greatest sinner in the world'.[59] The basic spiritual experience into which St John of the Cross wishes to lead others is then first and foremost an 'awakening of God in the soul'—and he later amplifies this, saying that, 'It is the soul that is moved and awakened.'[60] It is, therefore, an awakening of the person to the deepest truth of his or her being, namely that God's 'Yes' is indissolubly there in that person's life, even if, as St Thérèse of Lisieux (1873-97) puts it, 'I had committed all possible crimes'.[61]

Other spiritual authors such as John Tauler, St Teresa of Avila, Madame Guyon and Gerhard Tersteegen speak of

---

[58] *Summa Theologica*, II-II, quaestio 83: *Oratio est proprie religionis actus.*

[59] *Ascent of Mount Carmel*, II 5: 3.

[60] *Living Flame of Love*, 4: 2-6.

[61] *St Thérèse of Lisieux: Her Last Conversations*, 11 July 1897, trans. John Clarke, ICS Publications, 1977, p. 89.

'interior prayer'.[62] What they mean by this is praying from within; again, therefore, a conscious personal turning of the self towards God, from 'I' to 'You'. As was mentioned in Chapter 1, prayer for St Teresa means living with God as with a Friend and 'taking time frequently to be alone with him who we know loves us'.[63] Another expression frequently used in the spiritual tradition is 'the practice of the presence of God'. What is meant is that same fundamental act of faith: a real and at the same time completely simple action of the heart, one which everyone can do. It means that I am aware that this is the reality in which I believe, that God is there—and that in God's 'Yes' to us 'we live and move and have our being'.[64] Even if hidden, God is as truly there as any other person who is present. Then follows the *real* step. I speak to God, from within, so that it is really I who am speaking. I say 'You' to God, to this incomprehensibly great God, about whom I can only speculate. Then not only does our understanding say 'You', but this also comes spontaneously from deep inner places. Out of saying 'You' comes a turning from one being to the other, a looking upon one another, a waiting upon the great mystery which lovingly surrounds me and all existence, so hidden, and yet at the same time so close.

Taking seriously our faith that God is there

For all teachers of the Christian spiritual life, being one with God means really taking seriously our faith that God is there; not just talking about God, thinking about God and saying our prayers in God's presence, but maintaining a relationship with God; not just belonging to the Church, but listening to God; not just going about with a religious philosophy in our

---

[62] I have written on the meaning and the history of the expression 'interior prayer' in my little book, *Was ist inneres Beten?* 2nd ed., Vier-Türme-Verlag, Münsterschwarzach, 2002.

[63] *Life* of St Teresa, 8: 5.

[64] Acts 17: 28.

heads, but with the hidden yet present God as Friend and Partner, going through daily life in reverence and deep trust. And when spiritual teachers speak about the way of union, they are trying to say that this union is a way, and it therefore represents a developmental process, a movement into an ever deeper and more consciously lived being-one with God, which will one day reach its completion at the endpoint of life. Following the path of union means growing into a committed relationship with God as one grows into a friendship, letting oneself be formed step by step by this friendship, learning to see the world through God's eyes, making God's will (that is, God's attitude, spirit, thinking and feeling, ethics, character) more and more one's own.

It is not about some special spiritual path within the Church, but about the form of life which is meant if we speak of faith in the original—biblical and early Christian—sense, simply of the Christian way of being human. It is the way of committed relationship with God, where we are borne up in the trust that God is turned towards us in love, that God is always one with us. This path is also at the same time the path of union with our fellow human beings.

7.

A way of life in relationship with God

Jesus prays for our union with God

'Father ... that they may all be one. As you, Father, are in me and
I am in you, may they also be in us, so that the world may believe
that you have sent me.'[65]

'Jesus looked up to heaven and said ...'

WE SHALL NOW look at a few sentences at the conclusion of
these long farewell discourses. Chapter 17 often bears the title
'the farewell prayer of Jesus' or, as Martin Luther called it,
'the high priestly prayer of Jesus'—a term which has also
become widespread across the Christian denominations. The
prayer begins with the words, 'After Jesus had spoken these
words, he looked up to heaven and said, "Father ..."'[66] Jesus
lives with this Abba-God in an interior relationship of love
and friendship which characterizes his thinking about himself
and others and his way of dealing with people. The text
continues, 'I ask not only on behalf of these'—and here the
writers would have imagined Jesus looking round at the
disciples in the room at the Last Supper—'but also on behalf
of those who will believe in me through their word'.[67] We too
are included.

'that they may all be one'

Next come familiar words which we should try to hear as if
they were entirely new to us: 'Father ... that they may all be
one.' We have been accustomed over the decades to hearing

---

[65] John 17: 21.
[66] John 17: 1.
[67] John 17: 20.

41

these words chiefly in connection with ecumenical concerns—at ecumenical services and in prayers for the reunion and unity of Christendom. The encyclical of Pope John Paul II on ecumenism in 1995 bears the title *Ut unum sint*, or 'That they may be one'. In this age of ecumenism, these words are now usually understood as Jesus' prayer for Christians of different denominations to be one with each other (even though perceptions as to the appropriate nature of this unity may vary). The words give expression to the deep longing for unity. This way of understanding the verses is, however, relatively new: only as ecumenical concerns became increasingly important in about the 1930s and 1940s did Christians begin to understand and interpret the verses like this.

Unity with one another is undoubtedly one of Jesus' abiding concerns, and it is right to pray, 'Father, that we Christians may all be one', however we imagine unity should come about. Nevertheless, more precise study of the biblical text has made it clear that this is not actually in the text. Jesus is not speaking here about unity amongst or within the Christian denominations—that would not even have been in his thoughts at the time. Nor is he speaking about unity in situations of conflict and threatened division between different groupings in a community. In fact Jesus is not—at least at the most immediate level—speaking about unity between people at all. Biblical scholarship confirms that people in the past were right to understand these words as Jesus' petition for unity between God and the individual, as being about our relationship with God. We need to lay aside our ecumenical spectacles and listen again afresh to the text in the way intended by those who wrote it down.

'as you, Father, are in me, and I am in you'

In the works of St John of the Cross, for example, we find many wonderful reflections on the subject. St Thérèse of

Lisieux († 1897) and Blessed Elizabeth of the Trinity († 1906) also understood these verses in the way originally intended. Blessed Elizabeth wrote in a letter:

It seems to me that I have found my heaven on earth, since heaven is God, and God is [in] my soul. The day I understood that, everything became clear to me. I would like to whisper this secret to those I love so they too might always cling to God through everything, and so this prayer of Christ might be fulfilled: 'Father, may they be made perfectly one!'[68]

'Clinging to God' is the fundamental concern of Jesus in his farewell prayer.

When teachers of Christian spirituality speak of union with God, they do not mean extraordinary religious experiences, or even a (monistic) merging into the divine, as might initially suggest itself in our times, characterized by a plurality of religions. In Christian spirituality, union with God means taking seriously the belief that God is there, and therefore living in a condition of relationship with God. This is the way of union or the *via unitiva*, one of the aspects of the threefold way mentioned in Chapter 2. Christian spiritual teachers derived the way they referred to this essential aspect of the way of faith from the farewell discourses of Jesus, specifically the farewell prayer.

If Jesus had some unique characteristic for those who travelled around with him through the various regions, through Galilee and to Jerusalem, getting to know him more and more, then it was that deep in his heart he lived not a solitary existence, but with an inner 'we'—'You, Father, and I'—and that this inner 'we' made up his personality. People sensed that this was his centre, the source of the power which went out from him and which made everything possible—

---

[68] *Complete Works of Elizabeth of the Trinity*, Vol. 2: *I Have Found God: Letters From Carmel*, trans. Anne Englund Nash, Letter 122 to Madame de Sourdon, soon after 15 June 1902, ICS Publications, 1995, p. 51.

how he met and dealt with people, how he talked and what he did, how he was.

'may they also be in us'

The next phrase touches upon something which is also part of interpersonal relationships, a 'from me to You', when two friends who love each other really meet one another in mutuality and equality. 'As you, Father, are in me and I am in you, may they also be'—next we might have expected in you, but instead—'in us'. Jesus and the Father stand here as equals. That reflects the experience of life and prayer of those who wrote these texts and who had long believed and been aware that Jesus was alive; not just anywhere, but with God the Father; not just anywhere with the Father, but in this deep inner 'I-You' union. They believed, too, that when they turned to God the Father, they at the same time met Jesus Christ the Risen One living with the Father, and they therefore added, '[so] may they also be in us' (not in me).

Later on in the history of the Church, the express belief in the God who is Three-in-One develops. What Jesus prays for here is that we—each one of us, with his or her own name, I, Reinhard—find our way to an inner relationship with this God, that we say 'You' to God. Jesus is praying that God may not just be some object of belief in my head, some component in my philosophy of life and in my thinking, but that I, just as I am, turn personally to the hidden yet present God in whom I believe, take seriously that God really is here, and say, '*You, God*', just as Jesus did in his life.

'so that the world may believe that you have sent me'

If we do nevertheless look at the words, '… so that the world may believe that you have sent me' in terms of justifiable ecumenical concerns, then the interpretation more familiar to us emerges: 'If the Christian denominations were really one again, then the world would believe, "Yes! Christianity has got it right! They have found the right way!"' It might be a good thing if we took a few minutes for sober reflection—a few seconds are actually enough!—and asked ourselves if the world really *would* believe, when it saw what was going on amongst us. If we look at the text and understand it as originally intended, then we become aware of a far deeper meaning. It is not just about belonging to the Church and taking part in its life, but about attempting to live in deep personal intimacy and friendship in my heart with the God in whom I believe. It can become a way of leading a human life which inspires and appeals, which gives others the feeling that this is how they must live too, that there is something here which attracts and which radiates out life.

'The glory that you have given me, I have given them'

'Glory' is the word chosen by Jesus for this great and precious thing, this relationship with his Abba-God, this personal interior life, which shapes everything anew and radiates through all interpersonal relationships, and which he wishes to reveal and give to people. This is the meaning of the Kingdom of God for Jesus: life in its fullness, living as a twosome with the Father, and it is the concern of his heart that everyone discovers this glory. Only then do we find that which most deeply gives dignity to human life. God is, however, hidden from us, and it was just the same for Jesus. Jesus did not see God face to face in this life, and he had no other interior experience of God than we ourselves have. He lived with the Father who is hidden, yet present.

Even if we pray a great deal and we go to church on big feasts, or even every day, it is possible for it all to remain purely external and to bypass God, in reality having nothing to do with God. Union with God means that I personally and entirely genuinely turn to, and share my whole life with, God; that I tell—preferably in my own words—exactly what is going on in my life, about the concerns of my fellow human

45

beings, the joys and sorrows, everything. I turn to God and share it all, as I would with a friend, knowing that whatever I may get up to, God is my great Friend, who shares my life.

It is not enough just to say our prayers when attending a service, or at home, even if we do address God as 'You, God', as this is still too external. It is not about just saying with my lips, or thinking with my head, or reading out loud, 'You, God', but about this also happening within. It is just the same in an interpersonal relationship; it is possible to be with another person all day, and even to talk the whole time, but not really to meet the other for a single second. Failing to meet one another happens so often in our lives. We can also fail quite spectacularly—even when immersed in a church service—to meet God. It is possible to have the most splendid, even the very highest, roles in the Church, or to become very active in the parish, but in the process to fail to meet God. One can pray a great deal, yet nothing is really going on with God.

It is not necessary to pray for any longer than I currently do, or to increase my quota of prayers. I just have to *think about* God when I pray. It's about the quality, not the quantity of my spiritual life. I don't necessarily have to take more time for God, but I do have to take God more into my time—into my prayer time (!) and my work time and my free time—into both 'action' and 'contemplation'.

Prayer is also connected with keeping an inner place of remembrance within our hearts. We may think here of the detailed provisions in the Book of Exodus for keeping a day of remembrance of the Passover,[69] and the words which Jesus used at the Last Supper, 'Do this in remembrance of me.'[70] Just as one thinks about a friend who is not there and closes one's eyes, becoming interiorly aware of the other, imagining

---

[69] Exod. 12, esp. v. 14: 'This day shall be a day of remembrance for you.'
[70] Luke 22: 19.

46

that person, really making him or her present as if he or she were there, so one can also do this with God. And then we can speak to God, or just be silent. What we say, and how much we say, is not what matters.

We tend to seek out God when driven to do so by some need, when we want something, but for Jesus, God isn't the great helper in time of need, the wonderful feeling that there is someone is heaven to whom to turn for help. It is *God* who is of tremendous worth for him, rather than the hope of being able to ask for something and get it.

'that they may become completely one'

Jesus then says, 'I in them, and you in me, that they may become completely one.' Completion or perfection for Jesus is not about always getting everything right or not making mistakes. Jesus knows that we human beings can't be perfect. Christian perfection, as St Thérèse of Lisieux once said, does not consist of being perfect but of perfectly accepting one's imperfection. Jesus relates being complete, being perfect, to this unity with God.

We need here to be clear about how the people of the time, the ones who listened and the ones who wrote it down, understood 'completion' or 'perfection'. This was an important concept in the Greek and Roman world. Everyone wanted to be perfect. The Greeks and the Romans understood being perfect above all as external perfection, as being in the best possible condition through exercise, as being fit as a fiddle, having a body which looked good. For the Jews, perfection was the ideal of knowing by heart the Ten Commandments and the 634 individual commandments of the Torah, so that they could be recited at any time, together with having an understanding of them and keeping to them. Our text has to be understood against this background, and then we can see that today's ideals of perfection may have some connection with those of the Greeks and Romans and the Jews of that time. The times can in fact be very similar, because people remain the same.

Jesus says, 'that they may become completely one'. That is far more worth striving for, and even if we are not necessarily the healthiest, best-looking and fittest people, or in the best possible shape through exercise, or people who always do everything precisely according to rule, we shall have that for which Jesus here prays so longingly for us, that which for him is glory.

This way of living with God, this way of living out being human, will also of course have its consequences in our life together. If, however pitifully I succeed, I try to live with God in an interior union like this, then I discover of my own accord that I must also try to live in unity with others, and I see where living together is not working out as it should, or where there are tensions or blocks, since those things mar my relationship with God. Experience teaches us only too well that sustainable unity with one another can only come about where it involves union *with* God, and that this is the pre-condition for finding unity *in* God. Somehow both things belong together. From that perspective, it is right also to understand these verses as the way to unity between the denominations, in our families, or wherever, but we shall not achieve unity through setting up appropriate organizational methods, through making suitable alterations in the structures, through reworking everything. That can be important too, but it comes in second place.

Unity grows where people are trying to be one with God and then spontaneously become aware that, as they have a mutual Friend, so they must also try to live together in friendship. Union with God and union with one another belong together. The basic attitudes and dispositions which are valid for the one are also valid for the other. The fundamental activity of loving God is also the fundamental activity of loving our neighbour. Following the way of Jesus

48

means turning towards our fellow human beings in just the same way as we do to the hidden yet present God, with an attention which comes from within. It means not doing this just by works of charity (which remain external) and a kind word now and then, but with a simple 'activity' of the heart which looks upon the other and really *means* that person, consciously says 'You' to him or her, speaks, listens and spends time in his or her presence. What makes people into brothers and sisters is nothing more and nothing less than this simple looking at one another.

Living in relationship with God and believing we are loved, as Jesus knew himself to be loved, will also affect our relationship with our fellow human beings—not only with our brothers and sisters in other denominations, but beyond the boundaries of the Church—and our witness will have more power to attract others.

'so that the world may know
that you have loved them, even as you have loved me'

We expect to have a conversation with another person, but often think God is silent. As was said in Chapter 4, God does speak; if not audibly, yet in a language we can understand. Try to be still for a time, to be completely aware of this union with God, with the risen Jesus Christ, and to imagine:

Jesus, you are right here now, not somewhere far away. You are always with God, and you are here now. St Paul says we live in you, we move in you, we have our being in you. You are around me and within me. I live in you, and you in me. I'm trying to make myself more aware of this. I want to call you my Friend, to talk to you in my own words. I'm trying to believe what you say—and sometimes it's very hard to believe—that I'm not only worth something, but I'm of enormous worth to you.

Sometimes it is hard to believe, because from the time we were small children we have—to a greater or lesser extent— had some experience of feeling utterly worthless, or that we were only of value to the extent that we could accomplish things. This attitude can really bedevil and put its stamp on us, so that we have little belief in ourselves.

> Jesus, I want to believe that I'm worth something, that you call me your Friend, that you are here in my life and always with me. I will try to tell you about my life, about what is happening today, what I am thinking and feeling. Jesus, may we be one, as you have desired, both for me and for my fellow human beings.

'Father, I desire that those also ...'

'Father, I desire', Jesus prays, 'that those also, whom you have given me, may be with me where I am, to see my glory, which you have given me because you loved me before the foundation of the world.' It is all about a God for whom I am of incredible value from the first moment of my existence, and about Jesus praying with great longing for this union and this glory, that I, even I, Reinhard, who have been loved from the beginning with an unbelievably great love, will—at least now and again—look to God.